18 YEAR OLD , 80 YEAR ADVICE

Mr Danish

BLUEROSE PUBLISHERS
India | U.K.

Copyright © Mr Danish 2024

All rights reserved by author. No part of this publication may be reproduced, stored in a retrieval system or transmitted in any form or by any means, electronic, mechanical, photocopying, recording or otherwise, without the prior permission of the author. Although every precaution has been taken to verify the accuracy of the information contained herein, the publisher assumes no responsibility for any errors or omissions. No liability is assumed for damages that may result from the use of information contained within.

BlueRose Publishers takes no responsibility for any damages, losses, or liabilities that may arise from the use or misuse of the information, products, or services provided in this publication.

For permissions requests or inquiries regarding this publication, please contact:

BLUEROSE PUBLISHERS
www.BlueRoseONE.com
info@bluerosepublishers.com
+91 8882 898 898
+4407342408967

ISBN: 978-93-6261-218-2

First Edition: April 2024

PREFACE

Hi, beautiful readers before diving into the book and gaining the knowledge on all aspects of life, allow me to introduce myself to you. I am Mr Danish. I am a 18 year old (while writing this book) motivational speaker, live coach, trainer and mentor. I was 16 years old When I started my journey from confusion to building my dream and developing as a worthy individual. I have written everything in my book. This book is written with knowledge printed with love and delivered with a hope. A hope to make the world a better and best version.

PROLOGUE

A day with a bright sunshine starts and far away from the town, where two young guys sit and discuss about their life goals, dreams, aspirations, but this story isn't about dreams. It is about surprising friendship. That's going to change everything. The friendship with book. The two guys were walking around when they bumped into an old man sitting and was thinking something as if it was remembering something by watching these young guys, the guys also did notice him. He had some book or Journal filled with lots of experience which he called the guys and handed them to read. the journey begins here..

DEDICATION

Pari and jawa !!

Thanks to all my For love and with Love

family , friends and well wishers

ACKNOWLEDGEMENT

For all the ones who inspired me and was by my side when i am on this journey ..

CONTENTS

Preface iii

Prologue v

Dedication vii

Acknowledgement ix

1. Self Discovery 13

2. Desire 17

3. What is Life ? 21

4. Passion or Profession ? 25

5. The Start 29

6. Truth of Time 39

7. Reality of Goals 45

8. Honesty is the best Policy 51

9. Mindset Matters ? 55

10. Never Give Up ! 61

11. Learning is Overrated ? 67

12. Facts on Confidence 71

13. Hard Work or Smart Work ? 75

14. Action Action and Action 79

15. The RESTART 83

1. SELF DISCOVERY

The day a person is born , A lot of dreams and goals are born with him. The way a person is treated until his young age would have already shaped his thoughts, ideas, beliefs goals, its upbringing until the young age would already have decided how big he she dreams and how big his her aspirations. Life at 18 is like standing at a place where there are lots of roads going to different directions, each direction will permanently change your destination. A lot of roads, diverge here and each diversion has its own mini diversions. So deciding the road that leads to the destination You always wanted needs self discovery guidance Knowledge and also a little patience. Understanding oneself is the most important thing before we start any journey or take any road. what do we need? Where do I want to see myself when I turn back? Where do I want to reach? What is my destination? Are the most important questions which can only be answered when we understand ourselves. Every individual is completely different from another. His birth upbringing, life experiences, his challenges and victories, sacrifices and achievements, thinking and thoughts , Beliefs and actions are different, which clearly means to understand oneself It can only be done by the individual himself, but before diving into understanding zone, let's understand what actually is self discovery. Is it to know all the answers ? Or to have knowledge about the exact roadmap ? Self discovery is not about the above, but to understand that you may always not have answers. You may not always have guidance. You may have to take your own decision and work on it for hours, but you need to keep going and moving forward, whether whatever maybe the situation or circumstances. Weather whatever challenges you face when you discover that you have to Keep moving then You never stop that the first thing about self-discovery, which should be common for every individual, irrespective of life, experiences, and beliefs. Life is an enormous book and every day each morning is a new chapter, waiting to be written by your own hands and minds. Imagine you are in a bookstore surrounded by countless books representing the stories of different people. Each book holds different lessons experiences stories. Similarly, boring it could be having the same story or the same life. life is about trying the things making mistakes and learning along the way self discovery is a journey and not a destination. It's about finding out what makes your heartbeat a little faster. What makes your eyes light up with excitement it's about understanding that the process itself is where you find the most profound lesson, so my friends as you navigate through the pages of your own book, embrace the uncertainty, try new things take on challenges and learn from every twist and turn. Remember, your story is unique and it's okay, I say completely okay to not have it all figured out right now Or at once. remember the only reason you are taking the road to explore and find out to experience and make yourself more worth of being the best one. The more you walk, the more clear your vision will get , the more you walk the more stronger you become.

2. DESIRE

For the start of anything, a burning desire or a desire to achieve something is very important,. You cannot start anything or set for any takeoff until an unless you don't have a desire. Desire is a deep feeling or an emotion to achieve something that is connected with your heart or either with your mind. Desire is the starting point of any goals and any dreams that you think about. Without a burning desire, a person is never ready to put his hundred percent efforts in anything that he is up to achieve. Desire starts the journey. There in your mind and your heart, there should be a burning desire to achieve your goal. The goal should be as important to you as it's the only thing that you can do. There should be a desire that can overcome challenges. There should be a desire that can overcome failures, there should be a desire that is so deep that you are ready to put your hundred percent efforts and all the required sacrifices that your goals and your dreams demand. All the great things which are achieved in the world have started with a desire. It is the force that pushes you to achieve your dreams and your goals with the highest energy and efficiency. It is the force that trains, your mind and your heart, that understands the demand for your goal and your dreams, and then ignites you to start working for that particular dream. Desire helps you in overcoming any toughness or odds that you will face on your way to success. Whenever you dream about anything, the first step that is taken subconsciously or consciously to achieve that goal consist of a strong desire to achieve that. A desire to become successful, a desire to earn money, a desire to have a luxury life, nothing starts with a huge desire. It is important to note and understand that when you are on this journey, you will face several difficulties and lots of toughness. You will face hundreds and thousands of challenges on your way. Things will always go odd and you have to always think about, the end goal that you are going to achieve. If the end goal is as burning as your desire is, then you will overcome the challenges , the difficulties, the toughness with a smiling face, but if your desire is weak, then it can be thrown away with few challenges or odd. As we all know and understand that the path we are selecting or the goal we circumstances, but a strong desire to achieve that goal will act as a ray of light in the darkness. It shall motivate you whenever you feel low. It keeps you going even after a lot of failures. Therefore, before starting anything ignite in yourself the strong desire to achieve your particular goal. Find out why you need to achieve what you need to achieve. Find out the reason behind achieving or selecting a particular goal. Understand your WHY. The WHY behind your thoughts , the WHY that is pushing you towards your particular goal. The more you understand your WHY and the more stronger your WHY is to achieve that particular goal, the more chances is to succeed in that particular goal. The WHY of your particular goal is directly connected with your desires. How badly you need to achieve that goal. How eagerly you are waiting for that goal to be achieved and how dedicated and committed you are towards achieving your dream and success, are the important questions which can be solved with your WHY. When you have a reason to do what you are doing, when you have a reason to define your goal, When you have a reason to achieve any particular particular goal, then the goal and the dream becomes easier and meaningful to achieve. Find your WHY..

3. WHAT IS LIFE ?

Life, the small word has endless meanings and possibilities. Life is to live just before we delve into anything It is most important for us to understand first what life is the very first and scientific thing we can think of is , life is the air we breath , the heart that beats up , the eyes that see, but when we dive deep in life, we understand that life isn't just about being alive. It's about the actual practical experiences that we get during this journey. Life is like a big adventure. We are all part of this. it's ups and downs. It's shocks and surprises. Everything has its own meanings and worth. People have always wondered about the meaning of life, thinkers, poets, and smart people and we we have always tried to figure out what life is, but it turns out what makes life meaningful is different for each person. It depends on what we believe in , what is important to us and the things we have been through. the situations that made us the surprises that broke us. I believe myself that the meaning of the life is very subjective for every individual and it's even subjective based on the situations, ages and goals. When I was a small child for me, life was to just get maximum possible time to play, but when I was a grown-up kid, writing some exams and looking far away from the window for me, life was to just explore the different places and bunk the school . When I am a grown-up teen life is to have goals and fail in that so as to succeed further. when age changes the life and its meaning changes , only because we define life from our current thoughts, knowledge, experiences, and current priorities, but remember life is more than this life is to live itself, not just to exist. Life is to fail or win, but not to just to sit without any movement . as self discovery is a journey ,The life is similarly a journey to experience. There will be a lot of situations in life , That would not be welcomed but you and I have to go through them because they give us the most important lessons. The highest paid teacher in the world is our experience because we pay it with our most valuable things or emotions. Life is something between good and bad. It is something between happy and sad. It is something between success and failure, it is not always meant to have victory, but if we work towards certain goal, not that was more beneficial, but you didn't knew , the life knows about it. Why do we always tend to have everything answered. It is completely fine to not have answers at the very same moment. Because every journey we start is uncertain every plan you make will surely have some changes every road you take to reach certain destination will have some twists and turns , but it is all about to start the journey. imagine a dark night , and you have to reach a destination of thousand steps. You have a lamp in your hand. Is the lamp showing you the complete path, no ! Is it either possible to say that you will only start the journey when the complete path from step 1 to thousand is visible. A big no. but you can see that once you start taking the step, the lamp makes visible the next step. similarly, when you take the another step, the light of the lamp lightens up the next step exactly how the criteria of life is when the journey is started. It's completely fine to not have everything figured out, but when you keep moving towards the destination, you learn lessons , you make connections ,You gather experiences , You find your well wishes, You will fail , You will get cheated, but once you decide not to stop and continue the journey, you will face challenges, but you will never stop. You will reach your gets defeated and every time stands back again. It is easy to win against a person who tries, but it is hard to win against a person who keeps trying. Kisi bhi cheez ko krne me aur karte rahne me bhaot bada fark hota hai. Which means to do something and to keep doing something has a great difference . Many of these things seems to simple when we read it or listen to it. They seem to be very small things, but in reality, small things make extreme difference. a small hole in a very big and luxury ship can drown that ship. Similarly, a smile, a seemingly small and effortless experience holds the power to brighten someone's day. The small gesture creates a positive atmosphere fostering a sense of connection and warmth leaving a long lasting impact. So it's important to consider small things in life and get on this journey to explore and experience which itself is called life. Just read it twice ; Life is to live, not merely to exist.

4. PASSION OR PROFESSION ?

As , I have noticed this generation is struggling with two different things. One could be the career choose by their guardian and other is their passion, but before we could start for this journey, let's understand what passion is. There are many and subjective definitions for passion. Anything that ignites our souls, pushing us to perceive. Our dreams with unwavering determination could be said passion. It is the force that eliminates the excuses and barriers between you and your dreams. It is the light that enlighten the path and motivates us to reach towards the goal. Passion is something you love to do. It is something you work with gratitude. It is something that your interests and knowledge favours with, but when we say that passion use kahete hai jise karne me maza aata ho we also have a side that ki ap har din agar koi cheez don't learn something new or fresh. Passion is a part of your dream and not the dream itself. It is okay that you don't feel passionate about something or anything, it is completely okay. It is not possible for everyone to have a passion on guaranteed basis, you can still try to figure out your passion by exploring and giving a try to various activities. someone's passion can be exploring the world and others would love to research by sitting in a room on their laptop. Someone would love to play sports and others would love to study some love to paint and others are passionate about singing, anything that is making you comfortable can be your passion. Now You need to figure out whether if your passion can earn money for you. If yes, then it's your call. You can continue working on your passion and make money while happily living your passion, if your passion cannot earn for you, you then need to decide what possibly could be your profession. A simple meaning for profession could be what work you will be doing to earn living. It can be job or business, but the motive of it is to earn a living for you, and while practising your profession, you can actively enjoy your passion, similarly, if your passion can earn for you, you can also go for a profession and passion both which will result that both your passion and okay, not to have passion , you can explore various things and figure out whether you really don't have the passion or just haven't figured it out. Once you start trying and exploring various things you can know what works for you and what no. In case of not having anything passionate, it's not something to be sad about, I would say it's a great opportunity. You are like a empty book. You can write whatever you want in that book, you can do anything and learn anything that is beneficial in the society and for your personal growth. A empty jar can be filled with juice or dirty water. That now depends on you. When you start learning any of the subject you start developing interest in it, which will further force you to learn that subject deeper and become renowned about that particular subject. As we understood that passion itself is important and profession too. On the other hand, it is never about choosing one from both. It's about choosing the both so that the best results may reach you.

5. THE START

Anything you start in your life should surely come to an end. It is seen in most of the people, that they start various things. Be it gym or learning some skill or some work, but most of them end up leaving that in the middle and unsolved, which is very worst experience for your brain. we may think that it's a normal thing and nothing much to worry about, but when we try to dig deeper, we understand that when you set some goals for yourself and you leave that in the middle and if you do this repeatedly, it affects your subconscious mind. Your mind takes it as your incapability of finishing the goals that you make for yourself and your subconscious mind ends up making a belief that you will never be able to finish the goals that you set . which is a very disturbing belief for your mind that will affect your journey to make a better life. Therefore, it is very important for us to finish what we start so that we can end up getting either some result or some learning to enhance our life. The start of anything, let's say you decided to read 10 pages daily of some self help book. You first have to make that a routine and a habit so that you can continue it for long run. Habits are so important that they can either make you or break you. Good habits can make your life easier and successful. Similarly, bad habits can make your successful life a nightmare. Habits are to be given the importance. When we do something on regular basis, our mind understands it as a habit. HABITS can be defined as something or some activity that you do on regular basis. They can be good and bad Both. Now let me make it very clear that formation of both the habits required some amount of time and energy, but good habits can completely change your life to the positive directions, but bad habits, they seem good at the beginning as your dopamine hikes, but later it will give you endless damage if it is not directed on the right path. To understand if a habit is good or bad, You need to check out and think about the long-term results because most of the habits creates results in the long-term. For instance, reading a book for 10 pages daily will not make you a knowledgeable expert in few days or months. But that 10 pages if you read consistently for five years, you can become the expert of that particular subject, just 30 another example of eating some junk food. If you start eating junk food for few days, you will instantly not gain weight or feel sick or ill, but when you continue eating junk food, daily, even if a small amount , within a few months you will gain weight and you will no longer be able to maintain high immunity. These are the combined powers of consistency and habits . If the results are to come instantly, then everybody would go to gym. If results came instantly , Then everyone's dreams shall come true in just a week or so, but it's not the way. It is important to understand and realise that the powers and effects of our habits are long run, which are extremely powerful. You may have heard of a bamboo tree which grows barely to a extremely small height in five years, but after that, it grows at an astounding speed. Habits do take time until they reach a threshold. You need to be patient about it and understand the details of your habits. All your current situations are the results of the habits that you have followed till now. Your financial status is the result of your money spending habits. Your appearance and weight is the result of your eating habits. Your knowledge is the result of your reading habits, and you are the result of all your combined habits. Now when we talk about habits, there are two different things.

first one building good habits, require a change in self belief. The reason that you are performing your habit is the belief that you have to change , leave or develop any habit. Your first need to cater your beliefs. The way we understand ourselves and our habit is one of the most important thing. Our beliefs play a crucial role in doing anything . We may actively not feel the presence of our beliefs, but they are working behind Subconsciously . Beliefs build our identity and our identity decides how we are as a person. To build better habits ,There are several ways that can be followed. You can try to change your bad habits into the good one to start. For instance, whenever you remember about eating junk food, think about the long-term Image of yourself , fat man with several diseases and then instantly change your thought to eat something healthy, maybe fruits or vegetables. Similarly, whenever you perform any habit, do it consciously . Due to following the same activity for years, our mind have automated many of our actions. For example, whenever we enter a dark room, we ourselves without thinking directly switch on the light because this action has been automated by the mind. Similarly, there are many habits which or automated. For example, there may be any sofa in your house and whenever you sit subconscious mind. Changing them require to change the beliefs, so you need to be alert and conscious whenever you perform a habit , so you could know about it whenever you perform a habit. Let's say a daily routine. Write it all in a journal or a simple book and from them point out the good habits, the bad habits and the general habits like for instance, going to the gym for exercise is a good habit and wasting your time is a bad habit, but waking up is a general habit. When we note down everything of ours, we can identify them. The next thing could be to write down the time consumption of our habits, the amount of time that is consumed by each habit. When you try to get rid of the bad habits, you instantly can't do that. You need to go through the gradual process. First , you need to reduce the time of bad habits. For instance, let's say you are wasting three hours daily in watching some movies and you need to get rid of that. You can't say directly that I will not do it. You can start from reducing the time, try watching it for 2.5 hours for the first days and two hours for the another week and slowly reduce it to the level that you require. Similarly, let's say You wake up daily at 10 AM. You want to be awake early then don't directly set an alarm for 6 AM because you will be successful in waking up at at nine for another few days, and then you can start reducing it within the same procedure, and when we reduce the time consumption of bad habits note that you will have saved a lot of time, but if you do not make some good and healthy habits for the time, you will end up having another set of bad habits kyuki buri aadatein lagani nhi padhti vo apne aap lag jaati hai and that's the fact about habits, so it is better to dedicate that time for any particular habit. For either empowerment of knowledge, mental fitness, emotional intelligence, or spiritual fitness. This way will end up giving you more good and improvement habits that you ever had. When we have already dive deep into the habits , let us also talk on how can we get rid of our bad habits . Let's understand a simple, but a little complex context. When we think about a writer what comes in mind? The one who writes is a writer. Similarly when we talk about singer, what comes to our mind the one who sings is a singer the one who teaches is a teacher one who plays football or cricket is a player, so this concept tells us that what you do builds your identity. You are what you do it builds and makes your identity. If you are a failure, then you are going to waste your time. Get in the loop of entertainment will not learn anything will not improve.

need to have similar kinds of habits that should vote for the identity. Let's say you wanna quit the addiction of smoking. Don't say that I have quit smoking. Just say I am not a smoker. A small identity shift can train your subconscious mind to be your friend on this journey to build better habits. For the start of this journey as we have already understood that our environment build our thoughts. Our thoughts are converted into our actions. Our actions build our habits and our habits build our future. So while we build our good habits, it is also equally important to break the bad ones. As stated above , environment place a crucial role in building and breaking of the habits. Motivation can help you to start or restart, but a discipline of habits keep you going, and in this way of building good habits and breaking bad ones environment place an important Although passive role. Our habits are usually triggered by our environment. Usually we see that at some places, the price of plots and the flats are very high and at other places, the prices are low why it is like that ? Due to the environment. The plot or the flat can be same, but with a different environment, the environment where there are facilities a good locality , Well mannered neighbours or healthy and well-connected location will be high and on between ₹25. The same coffee at some restaurant would cost ₹100 rupees and at five star hotel, it may cost ₹200 and the coffee will be worth more than ₹350 at some airport. The coffee maybe same, but the price differ due to environment. This clearly states that how important is environment in most of the things. The kind of environment in which your upbringing took place would have influenced your believes and your thoughts about almost all the things. To break bad habits , It's important to first unlearn few concepts that have already taken your mind. A glass filled with water cannot be filled with juice because the glass is already full. To fill the juice, you first need to unload the glass with water. Similarly, there are many concepts that have already set up in your mind which always tends to seem correct, but they may not always be correct when we vision things with open mind and on the basis of facts, theories and researches. To break the bad habits , First understand the concept of environment whenever you are with a book or video or a person or group, it's already influencing your mind and lifestyle. Each minute you spend with someone or something creates changes in your mind, both conscious and subconscious, so it is important for us to choose our environment wisely. you should be very conscious about are going to be the sixth one. Whenever we are up for anything or changes in our life firstly consider that what environment could be beneficial for that. Bed is not for reading and table chair is not for sleeping, malls or not for education and colleges are not for shopping and entertainment. An aeroplane cannot fly from a railway station. Similarly, a railway station is not suitable for an aeroplane to fly. So we can well conclude that choosing a right environment is very important for both building and breaking of habits. The another concept is that to follow good habits , Each day make that good habit, easy to access and perform, make it worth of providing satisfaction and make it more interesting to perform, and on the contrary for the bad habits, make it very hard to access and perform. Create the list of negative outcomes of your bad habits in longer time, make it uninteresting , this way habits can play a significant role on your journey.

6. TRUTH OF TIME

Time, as we should know that it is one of the most valuable thing. At an early age, we always tend to have time for various things. But at an age of 30 to 50 or so We barely get time to do anything. So let us understand how time works and how can we make the time work for us. The generation of ours is taking time least seriously. We are underestimating the power of time. We have smartphones, sometimes two or even more, we are equipped with fair looking watches, but we never focus on the time that runs in them. The time that never stops the time that never comes back the time that has already gone. Time is not like any other thing. It is once gone, we cannot bring it back at any cost, it always goes and never stops for us or anyone be it a poor person or a millionaire. It is equally divided for everyone, irrespective of anything. It depends on us that how we utilise that time for our benefit and growth. If you do not run with time, you will be left back And everything will get developed updated, except you. Every second That is counting Will make you far away from your goals and dreams and aspirations. If you do not get up and work every second that moves will make you tired and feel worthless. we all think that time is free and it's a human nature that we barely respect free things, but it's not the case , time is not free. It is extremely worthy. Everything that you are losing by wasting the time is the cost that you are paying. Everything that you could have achieved if you did not waste the time, but couldn't achieve is the price that you have paid. Time is more worthy than we have ever imagined or thought. If you want to know the value of one second, ask it to the person who has just escaped the accident, if you want to know the worth of one minute, ask it to the person who just lost his gold medal in Olympics. If you want to know the importance of 10 minutes, ask the person, who has just missed his flight or train. To realise the value of an hour, ask the person who is waiting for years to meet his parents. To realise the value of a month, ask the person who wasted it only by saying I would do it from tomorrow in a better way. To understand the worth of one year, ask the person who has just failed his competitive exam. Every moment of your and my life is important and deserves to get our thankful to us. Let's not waste our permanent time on temporary things rather invest it on something that in future you could be proud of. Every second You gain knowledge and get better version is the building block of your upcoming life. We reap what we sow. So let's not waste our time on anything that is not use of and when we say we have to utilise our time properly, We don't mean that make us strict timetable and follow that without fail that is not worth and even not possible or practicable. That will make you mechanical machine. We are humans and not computers, when we say about making the best use of our time, we need to evaluate ourselves that how my last spent one hour is making me a better person. As simple as that. Ask yourself the day I spent today , how did it make me better version of myself? Did I learn something new that adds value to either my life or in the society ? Did I do something to make my future comfortable or did I just wasted in something that was not worth of? Ask yourself after every hour the above mentioned questions so that from now you can be alert and conscious. Know about your time that, from the 24 hours you get how much time is wasted in non-worthy things. Make a list of that and try to remove each and everything that is not interesting or you want to save your time then make sure you learn to say "no" to all non-important things. Some relatives call you to do something for instance , go to the market, without thinking we say yes or okay, but have you ever wondered this yes, is secretly destroying your future this yes will make you waste a lot of your time. Only because of the fear that if you don't say yes, they might get upset with you only because ki koyi bura na maan jaaye. You are not here to please each and every person the time and attention belongs to you. 24 hours are yours and not anyone else. Understand this. Use it the way that can make you a better person, the individual and a valuable human being, you say yes not for time wasting things, but in case, if something is important and urgent, that will also increase your value while saving a considerable amount of time. Similarly, the way we aggressively, use our phones and laptops. We don't even think and understand that how our days and months are finished just by passing the time and not working, even a single minute for our future goals and dreams. Whenever we are working on something or just spending our time, whenever we say yes to something whether is beneficial or not, we say no to other things, that may be beneficial. The time you spend unused affect you from two sides.

if you wasted your two hours in watching some entertainment, it's obvious that your two hours are wasted, but in that two hours, you could have gained some knowledge or made yourself fit , is also wasted. Therefore it is extremely important for us to utilise our time and invest it rather than spending it. Take time as it is your money or something more important. The way we do not waste our money in silly or un important things, the way we invest our money in the projects, schemes and that provides maximum benefits Similarly, we should ensure to invest our time in the way that can build our future as good as healthy as possible in all aspects. Time once used or go gone cannot be brought back as it is said popularly that even time doesn't have time to give you back the time. So we can conclude the time is the greatest aspect of our journey and being success in any of the form, make a proper mark of each minute. Ensure to make pre-day plans for the upcoming day with exact time and location that particular habit or action will be performed from this time to this time at this location so that there is no room for wasting the time, for instance, write that I will read 20 pages of a book from 11 AM to 11:45 AM at my study room. This will give you clear instructions on taking any action.

room for missing and finding an excuse to get rid from it. At the end of the day, analyse your day and the results, and your hard work. Analyse what you have done the day long. What you have expected and What was the reality, compare the both, and try making appropriate changes in your schedule and task list. By doing so on daily basis you will end up making a list that perfectly suits you, your mind, your heart, your goals, that will increase your productivity to the next level and can give you desired results about what you have thought to accomplish.

7. REALITY OF GOALS

We are building habits, managing our time, but for what ? To reach our goals. And what are our goals ? Do we know what exactly are our goals? Do we understand Our goals? Are our goals, realistic and achievable ? Are our goals worth achieving ? Are the important questions that arises. Goals are basically our aims and targets we set for ourself. They can be big goals or divided into small ones. But the first condition about setting a goal is, it should be extremely clear. The goals must be very clear and not bold statement. Example ; we say I wanna earn a lot of money. Is this a goal ? It is an incomplete written bold statement more like an emotion. Goals need to be clear, understandable dividable, achievable, and most importantly, time bounded. Whenever goal is understandable, our mind process it faster and directly hits our subconscious mind. Our mind will generate great ideas and techniques regarding achieving that particular goal. Similarly if your goal is divided, which means if it is capable of breaking into small goals, then it becomes easy, setting targets and achieving small goals to reach the ultimate one. It increases the chances for the achievement as it provides confidence, motivation and a sense of achievement. And while this process, when you decide an ultimate goal, make sure if it is achievable goal, few of us set the goals that are unrealistic for our current situation. So keep away from making such goals or you will end up losing confidence in yourself. Start setting your goals by recognising the available time you have, your life conditions, your health, and what you can do. When you start achieving your goals You can start increasing your targets and slowly get onto the bigger level. Remember like anything cannot be done instantly Similarly, are the goals. They required an ample amount of time to achieve. It is a process of actions. So decide a particular time for a goal. A goal is not a goal until it is time bounded or time restricted. What do you want to achieve, at What period of time, is the most important thing. For example, you want to learn some language, let's say German, if you do not restrict this goal to a particular time, perhaps you may have whole life to achieve that or even it is possible that you may leave this goal behind, and if you make clear instructions about have a clear achievable and time restricted goal. Now the first and foremost thing is to divide your goal into sects and various forms and make it a daily learning process. Goals are set once but processes are performed and updated daily without fail. Goals gives us a direction but process is what makes our goal achievable. Once you set a goal, don't stick thinking about it. Rather think about the process that can help you reach the goal. Goals should not be focused rather process should be focused. Merely setting a goal cannot help us achieve that. For instance 25 to 30 lakh students who are into competitive exams have a same goal, that is to crack that particular exam with leading marks. They have the same goal, but only top 2% are able to clear it. This is because they have the same goal but a different process. They have the same destination but a different path. This is where the difference comes in and plays an important role. Never think too much about goal. Once you have set it think about various processes and systems that can help you crack that goal. Various tricks and techniques, various ideas and innovations. This is how a goal is achieved. If we merely think about goal, we would never be able to figure out the process, it's true that your goal should be in your mind, but it should take only 1% of your mind pointers away from the opposition team, and the time is already burning, there your foremost task is to throw that ball into the basket and achieve a goal. Now what would happen if you stand still and keep thinking that you have to throw a goal you just stand and think. Nothing changes. Rather if you plan and strategise about it with Team and move forward, do whatever it takes and throw a basket. That is when the result you want comes, your points are increased. So this is how the goals and process work. When I say this do I say that goals are not much importance ? Goals are very important because they give you a direction and destination to reach. If I may ask you what is the most important thing required to climb the mountain ? Your answer could be fitness, good health, perseverance, courage, stamina, practice, but let me tell you that the most important thing required to climb mountain is mountain itself. Firstly you need to have a mountain to climb on it. Similarly to achieve anything or something or build any process you need to have goal itself. So therefore it is extremely important to set a goal but once you set a goal, your focus should be on the process and not on the goal. This is how the whole science of cracking the goal works. So start building goal for yourself and make strong process and systems drastic change in your life. It is a happiness for a day or a few, but your journey is ever going and everlasting achieving of any goal should not stop you from making another goal and achieving it. This will make your process and systems stronger that would make every going and achieving !!

8. HONESTY IS THE BEST POLICY

Being honest is one of the most important aspects. It is very wonderful that without being honest, you cannot reach any important goal. Whether you work extreme hard and smart or you make a well fashion timetable. You will end up reaching somewhere else. A question may arise that what honest is? And being honest to whom ? 1st to yourself, yes, first become honest to yourself. Our lives are in dark, and that is getting deeper. The only light we have is of honesty. Unless you become honest to yourself, you will always struggle to be honest about what you want in your life. Be honest about your abilities and strength. M any and many of us Tend to tell our parents lie about our studies and work. Don't we ? Even if we have wasted our day w n e say this lie that we were studying, even if we are watching some film out in honest about it and most importantly, whom are you lying? You are actually not Lying to your parents, but to yourself. For the sake of temporary relief you and we are playing with our future, the future we dream about, the future we want to build for ourself. The lie initially doesn't seem to be very huge, but continuing this will make you and habitual liar. Being honest is sometimes considered hard, but it is not. It is simple. Just say the truth to yourself. Be honest with yourself at least ask questions to yourself and find out that even if you are honest about your basics. Ask yourself that why are you doing what you are doing? What is the reason behind choosing and working for your goal? What is your why? Even are you even honest about that? Have you started this journey with your own interest or with the pressure of society or for the sake of completion of your parents dreams. Be honest about your failures and mistakes. Take the responsibility rather than blaming others, only then it is possible to move forward and think further. Many of us are writing competitive exams for years and failing each time. Deep inside ourselves, we know that how much hard we work even then we will not be able to crack that. Even then doing it just because of the pressure of parents or society or just to please others, and weakness. Your abilities and skills. Your knowledge and interest. Work on that. Say truth to yourself and start working on your strength so that the other day you can become master of that. Leave the lie. Don't be shy. Give your interest a try. If you feel so. The basics built with truth are much stronger than that of the basics built with lie, you can live to the fullest and give your best when you know about yourself as deep as possible, learn yourself and ask genuine questions and answer with honesty, and you will see that you are on the right path and things have become easy, clear and meaningful.

9. MINDSET MATTERS ?

Our body is completely controlled by our mind. Every second you think, any action you take, any decision you take, it is directly controlled by your mind. Our mind sends instructions to our body for each action. It can be surely said that a sound mind will have a sound body, therefore, it is important for us to develop our mind and build it in a structured way . Even in our mind, there are two levels. The conscious mind and the subconscious mind. 95% of our brain consist of the subconscious one another 5% is conscious mind. It is understood that 95% of our brain and actions are controlled by our subconscious mind. Now, the mindset is directly connected with our subconscious mind. To explain conscious mind, it is the active mind that acts actively and understands concepts, and whatever becomes habitual with the conscious mind directly sinks down towards subconscious mind that works passively. Every action we take, every word we speak, directly affects our conscious mind and the repetition of the same will make it to the subconscious mind. Our mindset has profound impact on our lifestyle. The way we perceive the world it influences our actions. some may find a bottle half empty and others may find it half filled. It depends on the mindset we have. There were these young boys who were just graduated from a college. They both went to the same company for the interview and job. The company sent the first boy in a town and told him to sell the shoes. The boy went there. He saw that in the town no one wears shoes so disappointed with this, he returned and reported to the manager that no one wears shoes there in the Town, so it is impossible to sell the shoes of our company, then the manager sent the second boy to the same town. The second boy went to the town and observed that there were no one who wears shoes. He thought for a while, and then phoned his manager. The manager thought that even this second boy would say that shoes can't be sold there, but when the manager listened to him, he was shocked. The guy said to the manager to send the whole stock of shoes to the town because in the town, no one has ever experienced the feeling of wearing shoes and it is a great opportunity for him to sell the shoes there. Everyone would love this company, same shoes, but the different mindset changes the whole game. Mindset can totally shift the situation from positive to negative or the other way round. Nazar ka ilaaj toh koi bhi kr sakta hai par nazariye ka ilaaj koi nhi kr sakta. They can treat your eyes but not your vision. This is how the mindset matters. Your mindset makes all the changes. Mindset can be defined as the collection of our thoughts, beliefs, our values, and wisdom that creates our perception about the world, some people may have a predetermined mindset about their abilities and strengths. They think and believe that the potential they have is prebuilt. Some have the mindset that their potential is limitless and can be developed with proper efforts and time. They believe that their strength can be used, their weaknesses made up, their skills be developed. All depends upon the mindset we build for ourselves. When we take decision upon building a mindset, remember to reframe it the best you can as the mindset will cultivate your future and influence all your actions not only in humans, but mindset plays a great role in animals as well. There was a boy who was travelling from one village to another village and on his way, he saw the group of elephants, the elephants legs were tied with a very small rope. And with just a small and easily breakable rope. If the elephants wanted, they can break the rope in a second, but no elephant were trying to break it. They were all just following the orders of their caretaker. When the boy went to the caretaker and asked that why are elephants not even trying to break the rope as it is extremely easy for them to do so. The caretaker replied, when the elephants were young and small, he used to tie their leg with the same rope. And as they were young and small, they were not capable of breaking the rope. They tried every day, but they were not able to do it. Days passed and they accepted that they would never be able to break the rope. They adopted the mindset. Even now when they grew huge, they never try to break it, thinking that they would never be able to do it. The mindset is already predefined. It would never change. Similarly, there are many people who have their mindset predecided and determined and already decided about their abilities and limits. With this mindset, you will never be able to grow in your life after one extent. The other mindset is the growth mindset. To believe that your abilities and strengths can be developed by working towards it. Your skills would get better with practice. Your weakness would fade up with time. Your mindset can be built and will always believe on themselves. They are ready to learn and grow. They are ready to put efforts and make changes. Your mindset will determine if you will make yourself or break yourself, your mindset will determine if you will be remembered by the people or you will be forgotten. Your mindset will decide whether you will be committed in achieving your goals even when things get tough. Your mindset is your greatest asset. Yes, it's worth more than any college degree or educational qualification , worth more than any investment or training. Every new day you are given many choices, the choice to take the easy road which can give you a common life or the road with hills and mountains. The road with rivers and wells. The road with ups and downs. The easy one would accept you as you are, but the tough one would demand a better you. The best version of yourself. It will want you to face and overcome challenges and reach your goal. Remember, taking tough road would give you a comfortable future, but choosing easy road now can make you end up with with tough life. So make better choices as it's all about how and what we choose. We always have choices. RIGHT and WRONG have five letters each POSITIVITY and NEGATIVITY have ten letters each, are totally opposite. No one has the right to choose for you. The choice is yours....

10. NEVER GIVE UP !

You are on a journey to do something extraordinary. So what do you think you are going to do this without any odds or failures? That seems impossible right? Yes, it is. Everything is possible in the world, but achieving success without failures is almost next to impossible. You will surely fail Not one time, but many times for different reasons on different plans by others or yourself. The one who can stand up again after odds is the person who will reach far away in life even more than his expectations. One should have NEVER GIVE UP attitude. No matter what the situation is, no matter how many challenges you face, no matter what people say about you just remember, never give up. If you give up then it's a guarantee that you will never reach your goal, but if you continue fighting with your odds, then there is a possibility that you will win. Your failures are the proof that you are trying. We always Tend to see the success of people, but we never see their failures. We see their Glam, money, fame, luxury, but we don't see their hard work, their sleepless nights, their breakdowns, their problems and challenges. Michael Jordan is one of the greatest basketball player of all time. Once in the interview, he was asked the reason behind his success. He replied that to reach this level, I have missed 9000 basketball shots and there were numerous times, when Team trusted on me for final basketball shot, but I missed it. These were the words of the person who is role model to many people. Behind the success of a person there are many of his failures with a never giving up attitude. Who among us doesn't know SRK, he is one of the most famous and richest actor in the world. When he was asked about his luxury and fame, he replied the same that people have seen the fame, but behind that there is a huge hard work each day. A person with knowledge can fail, a person with hard work can, fail a person with back support can fail, a person with talent can fail, but a person with NEVER GIVE UP attitude cannot fails. He learns. Learn something from your failure to reduce your loss. They are the best teachers you will ever get. By failing you have paid a price and in return, you will surely get a learning learn from it. What to do next time and what not to do so that you do not for all time. Some part of a mistake is always correct, so learn from that. Even learn from others mistakes. Life is too short to commit all mistakes so learn from the mistakes of others so that you shall not repeat the same and practice the things in a better possible way. It is the human mind pre-programming that it is designed in a way to keep you safe. Therefore, it always rejects getting out of the comfort zone. It always forces us to be in our comfort, but great things cannot be achieved from comfort. They are achieved from failures. These failures and battles are preparing you for the upcoming achievement. Go and chase your dreams stand tall and show the world that what you dream can be turned into reality, if toughness tackles you down, get your reasons and get up again. If you look back to your life, you should not have regrets. Failures are better than regret. Trying is better than crying. Only you know your dreams and no one is better than you to chase it. You are more powerful than you could ever imagine. You are worth of achieving anything. Life will fail you sometimes and break you many times each time you take a bold step, you will see odds and toughness coming to your side. You may have heard the story of a frog who was fell into the well with other frogs. They were trying their hard to out were shouting for the frog who was struck. That you are not capable of doing anything. Nothing is possible for you. You are weak you are unskilful, but the other frog tried continuously and came out and what they find to their surprise was, the other frog was deaf and the frog was thinking that they were cheering for him. Why not we become deaf for few things and just do what we feel. So that best can be executed. Anything happens there will be a certain reaction. Someone will appreciate others may not, in both the cases you just need to keep going. You are doing good ? keep going. Doing bad ? Keep going. That's how simple it is. The main objective of yours should not be to listen to what others say (ofcourse your parents may be an exception) You need to figure out on yourself that what is making you more worthy each day and capable of accomplishing your dreams. I require you to increase your strength each day and the day will arrive when your strengths will be greater than your goals and you will see your goals accomplishing. Remind yourself of your WHY whenever you think about giving up. You have come this far for what just to leave your dreams in the way ? It has costed you reach here. You are after various setbacks and challenges. They are the part of our journey. How boring

!! The value of any of your achievement is decided by the challenges you faced while on your journey. The more challenging your journey is , the more high your success will be. Accomplishment of great goals needs time. So keep patience. A bottle can be filled with water within a minute, but a container requires hours. Don't be sad about the time it takes because results will be worth the time you spent on becoming something. Have patience and be focused on your goal. This can make you reach your goal even after several failures and odds, Enjoy the journey.

11. LEARNING IS OVERRATED ?

Learning is something that is never ending process. It lasts lifelong. Learning develops our brain and blesses us with a creative thinking ability. We always think that learning or education is only about what we learn in our schools or colleges inside the classroom. That is a theoretical learning, the practical learning starts outside of the schools and classrooms. Education is not only about reading and understanding various subjects. Yes, they are important too, but not the only thing we need to learn. Life teachers at every step. Learning can be done anywhere and everywhere. You can learn from anyone younger to you or older, richer than you or the poor, everyone has some good qualities and good is to be learnt, bad to be ignored. We never think about learning outside the classrooms. The world is developing at an

Educating yourself is as important as having Food daily. Food keeps you your body energised and alive. Similarly learning keeps your mind alive and energised. It develops various parts of your mind and opens up your mind with a wider aspect. Your thinking is developed to a greater level. Whenever a situation arises, you will be able to deal with it in a better way. You will be able to judge things with a broader perspective, people will Love to share time with you as your mind is more active, sharp and developed, as they dream. When your mind develops and you keep learning about various aspects for instance, discipline your manners, communication skills, other soft skills, your personality develops, and when you learn about various topics your personality shines people will love to talk and be with you. They will always value your time. They start considering about your thoughts. They will feel proud being your friend. You will notice that suddenly the value of your words start increasing and you are respected more comparatively. Learning and educating yourself has various external benefits and also a lot internal benefits. The confidence increases in yourself. The thoughts are developed and your energy on positivity is cultivated. Your sense of judgement and your calmness is furnished.

that there are infinite things to learn, and he will never become arrogant about his learning. Rather, it makes him a calm and a patient person. Learning not only makes you a better person for yourself, but also it makes you a healthy individual for the society. with all the learnings you have, you can bring a significant positive change in the society and help others to build themselves. The world today is growing at an extreme high speed. Various innovations takes place on the daily basis. Many things are updated. Various concepts are rebuilt daily. Not updating yourself with all these may force you to leave behind, even if you are working in any field, it requires the process of updating yourself on the regular basis, not doing so for a very long period may disconnect you from the latest and updated version of the world. Therefore, try enriching yourself with various knowledgeable aspects that could brighten your future and help you grow updated with better you!!

12. FACTS ON CONFIDENCE

Half of the battle is already won if you are confident about winning it. Confident is essential if you are up to anything. Most of the goals we set for a high-level of success are tough and walking on the path of that requires confidence. Before taking any decision requires a good amount of confidence. A very harsh reality about the era, we are living in is most of us are either overconfident or under-confident. Confidence is a skill that needs to be cultivated on a regular basis. Confidence increase the chance for success, which is obvious because when you are confident, you perform your actions with least pressure and highest focus. With confidence, you never take things lightly and prepare for it the best you can. And if you are into something that requires the judgement of others then confidence makes sure to make your way easier. It helps you overpower various failures and problems that could have broken you and kept you behind. But when we talk about confidence, there are three aspects one is confidence itself. The second one is overconfidence and the third one is under-confidence. Under-confidence and overconfidence, both are problems on your journey. Under confidence decreases our motivation level and makes our performance weak. Under confidence can affect the goals badly that you were capable of achieving. Even if you had skill, talent, knowledge and opportunity, you may fail only because of being under confident, therefore, one needs to develop the attitude of being confident. It is important for a growth mindset and positive lifestyle. It helps to trust yourself and gives you sense of control. With this trait vested inside you, you can face and overcome all the challenges of your life. Understanding yourself better, your weaknesses , your strengths, skills and Abilities will help you boost your confidence. Try to set tiny goals for yourself and when you achieve them, the self-confidence increases automatically the other way is to surround yourself in a positive and cheering environment who can boost your confidence and one more way to boost confidence is to try various new things that you fear about doing. These things will build your belief on yourself and your own skills. But when people get to their confidence, few or

In this state People listen to nobody and are always egoistic, there is a very small barrier between confidence and overconfidence. "I can crack the exam if I prepare well" is the confidence. "I don't need to prepare to crack such exams" are the words of overconfidence. "I will win the game" is confidence . "No one can win except me" is over confidence. Always analyse yourself, whether you are within the boundaries of confidence, or you have crossed them to reach the overconfident state. Usually people with overconfidence are blinded or don't see the abilities and strength of others and not their weaknesses which makes them lose. Be it a game, sport, conversation, exam or life. It always works like this. Being overconfident can make you ignore, not only your weakness, but also others strengths. Neither overconfidence nor under confidence. Just be self-confident. Confidence acts like your hidden power to do anything. Self confidence is all about believing in your own abilities and strengths. It is all about believing on yourself. Its true that its not always easy to do so. There maybe many setbacks and doubts. But to rise above that is confidence. We or no one is born with the skill of confidence. It is not something that has been given to few people, and others are left behind. It is a more like a important. It changes the whole situations. Many of the things are just based on your confidence. When you get out on this world, you require it at every step. Either you go to school or collage , office or at business meetings, the confidence should be visible shining from your eyes. The world is not here to trust you but at least you can trust yourself. Self confidence is it understand that you are not perfect but you are unique. No one is perfect but yes everyone is unique. You have your own set of skills and abilities. So trust your abilities and strengths. That will make you win most of it, try various new things, believe in yourself and achieve, celebrate various small goals. This will build self-confidence. Remember confidence is not optional, if it is, then is as important as the optional of UPSC.

13. HARD WORK OR SMART WORK ?

There is a good amount of confusion among two terms whether to work hard or to work smart. One of the most important thing to understand is success requires you to work hard and smart Both. Hard work is extremely important for any kind of success. The person who doesn't work hard will not reach much far in any of his goals, because you are competing with yourself each day and you have to grow every single day that needs a good amount of hard work. Now hard work does not mean that you are continuously working without sleep , without proper taking care of your health , without any plans. Hard work has a very simple and a very beautiful meaning, hard work means to give your hundred percent. That's the perfect definition of hard work. Just give your hundred percent in anything that you are doing. You are has their own situations. Everyone have their own problems. Everyone have their own solutions. Similarly, you have to figure out what works for you. You have to figure out what you are going to do with your goals. You have to figure out what your life will look like after 10 years. That all depends upon your hard work. Just try to give your hundred percent, on anything that you do. Your hundred percent will increase day by day. Today Maybe you can work for just 2 to 3 hours or you can think of 5 to 10 ideas. After a month, You may be able to work for more hours. That all depends upon how you increase your strength as the days and months pass. It all depends upon , how ready are you to compete with yourself and to defeat the yesterday's you. It all depends on how eagerly and how dedicated and how committed you are towards your goal. Commitment is one of the most important thing that is connected with hard work. If you are committed and dedicated towards your goal, then you shall work hard for that particular goal, but if commitment, dedication and hard work is missing, then it is like a incomplete story. When you start on any journey, you have to work hard. Because when you start, you might not have some talent or some skills or some opportunities, but the only option you have to start strengths. It's all about pushing your limits to the best you can. Similarly, when you reach a particular level while working hard, now you have to combine hard work with smart work because smart work is as important as hard work or you can also say that smart work is a little superior than hard work. When you start your journey the most important thing you can do is to work hard, but when you reach to a certain level, the best you can do is to work smart or else your development will be stuck at some level and you will not grow further. Smart work simply means to perform things in the best way they can be performed. There are always best and better options for various things to perform. Every plan has a upgraded version. Every every action you take can be done in upgraded way. Similarly everything you do should be done in a smart or or updated way so that the best results can reach you. Smart work is extremely helpful to significantly achieve various results or to significantly grow in your life. It brings drastic changes in lives of the people. Smart work usually involves making plans and performing things with highest efficiency and least labour force. Smart work saves a lot of our time and increases the quality of the results as it requires a good amount of planning, procedure and an they are transformed into the smarter way, The best example can be the transport. The transport was very difficult task as it was done with the maximum labour force or human force. But as the vehicles and technology is advancing, the transport have become extremely easy and reliable for all the people. This can be a good example to understand the difference between the hard work and smart work. Hard work usually, makes you committed and dedicated towards your goal. On the other hand, smart work saves a good amount of your time, and it provides you with the highest efficient and most structured results that can provide you a better amount of understanding and a good amount of learning. To conclude the both, we can say that hard work and smart works are both important at their respective times. Hard work plays important and crucial role while you are starting for any journey, but smart work becomes important and necessary when you need to upgrade and lift yourself with an astounding speed. Both have their own importance and contribution towards your journey, it is better for us to understand the situation and circumstances before choosing anyone of them or both of them. They have there own purpose and their own benefits that can be helpful at various situation but the

14. ACTION ACTION AND ACTION ..

Many of us are just in thinking or so-called overthinking mode. We never ever stop this. We have made the goals, the plans, but we are not taking actions. We know almost many things. We have a good amount of knowledge at least enough to make our life better compare to now, but knowing is not enough, nothing changes from knowing. Everyone knows that waking up early and having a jog can make their life better, but how many people actually do this? Everyone know that addictions are impacting our lives negatively, but what happens from knowing. Again, knowing something does not practically change anything. It is always action that brings the change and improves our lives. It is action that creates results. If you are dreaming of something and never working for it. Then the dream will ever remain the dream. It is not lead our life decides our future. If you want to change your results then you need to change your process. There are millions of peoples who know many of the things who knows how to improve health, they know how to cultivate wisdom, they know how to gain knowledge, they know how to lift a business, but what has changed, the condition is same. Nothing has improved. This is because they never act upon their theories due to various reasons, be it procrastination or some other barriers, but it's true that they never act. This is the difference between the people who grow in their life and those who are struck. Some struck because they want to do the things in a perfect way, I had one of my friend in school, he was always making some plans. He used to write that; when I buy this, I'll do that when I get this camera, I will record videos, when I read 20 books then I shall start implementation. He always used to write all this things with full of passion, but my eyes are witness, he never did any of the above and is still making some plans. Legends say he'll be always making some plans. Don't wait for the perfect time or place or equipment. just do it with whatever you have handy. Just act upon it. Don't wait or else your important phase of life would be vanished away, and you will never know. It is very actions and working upon it. You may have the knowledge of thousands of concepts , you may know many of ideas and action plans , but perhaps if you never convert them into your real life then you will lead the same life you are living and you can see no change around you and inside you as well. Everything starts with a dream, desire and goal but anything cannot be accomplished without being acting about that. Even if you know 100 secrets of fitness and if you don't apply it, then i doesn't have any weightage. Even if you have read 100s of books but you didn't implement even one of the formula then perhaps you are overweight in terms of knowledge. There are thousands of plans , formulas but it is necessary to understand what works for you. What is your cup of tea. You need to tailor those plans according to your goals and dreams and make a proper structured process yet simple to achieve your dreams. If you don't remind yourself everyday what you are becoming, by taking actions ; the world world will remind you what you are not. The fact about your dreams is that, only you can see it. If you want others to see that too, then you have to turn it into reality. To do so you have to work upon that actively. Even when you start doing so, you will face a lot of hurdles either from yourself or from the fear of not doing it in a perfect way. Or you may do it but may face some odds from other people saying that you can not capable of doing anything. With all these toughness your way, still you need to work upon your dream and goals. People are ready to say something on anything you do. Even if you do good you will have questions asked by them. Anything you do, it will not be able to please everyone and its not your duty either to please everyone. There will be someone with some problems. In most of the cases the problem is your vision. The problem is your vast thinking and big dreams for them. Remember when you are upto something great, it takes a lot to do that. Important thing to note that is to keep going and keep doing your work.

By taking actions you improve every day. Try to find your weakness and improve it, work upon it on daily basis, this will make your actions more superior and powerful.

15. THE RESTART

In whatever phase of life, you are, you are still capable of achieving the things that you have dreamt. All the things in the book may help you achieve something or make your life 1% better. In the end, I would say that many and many of the people read many and many of the books they watch several videos Thousands of pages, lakhs of advices, 10 lakhs of suggestions, but nothing changes because they never work and act seriously upon the information and the content they learn. So I would like to and love to remind you that whatever you have learnt, even if a single thing, just start implementing. Your life will change drastically and you will, find out that things are getting better around you. In the end I would like to say that on this journey just be happy because happiness is something that does not come from any achievement or result, yeah, that can be a happiness of few moments or few days, but that's not the permanent happiness. Being happy is skill itself. Being happy is the state of mind.

You can be happy at any situation. You can be happy with minimum facilities and still be unhappy with thousands of gadgets. so being happy is choice. You have to choose to be happy and just respect your parents, teachers, and elders. Remember first we need to become Human!!

www.ingramcontent.com/pod-product-compliance
Lightning Source LLC
LaVergne TN
LVHW061559070526
838199LV00077B/7109